North American
Endangered Species

By Colleayn O. Mastin 🐾 Illustrated by Jan Sovak

Grasshopper
BOOKS PUBLISHING

Black-footed Ferret

Near the burrows of the prairie dog,
The black-footed ferret once thrived;
Where prairie dogs set up a "town,"
The black-footed ferret arrived.

But prairie dogs' homes grew fewer
When their grasslands were taken away;
Then the black-footed ferret discovered
That it had no place to stay.

Before people came to the prairies, there were thousands of small, brown, burrowing prairie dogs, the favorite food of the black-footed ferret. When the prairie dogs seemed to be eating too much of the farmers' grass, they were killed by poisoning and hunting.

This led to the disappearance of the ferret. For as well as eating prairie dogs, these ferrets would often take over their burrows and make their homes in the middle of a prairie dog town.

Before ferrets became a seriously endangered species, the females would give birth to three to five young in late spring.

Today, the black-footed ferret is described as "the rarest North American mammal."

Cougar

The mountain lion or cougar
Is a sly and stealthy cat;
It truly is carnivorous,
Likes moose and things like that.

This solitary hunter
Is very hard to see
As it creeps through mountain forests
As hungry as can be.

The cougar is the largest cat in North America. This fierce cat is endangered in the eastern parts of both Canada and the United States, but it does seem to be surviving quite well in the mountains of western Canada and the United States.

Cougar skin and meat have little value, but a cougar pelt is often used as a trophy rug or wall-hanging. Hunting, trapping, poisoning and the taking over of its habitat by people are reasons that it is endangered. Other than humans, the cougar's only enemy is the wolf.

These solitary animals hunt and live alone, coming together only at mating time. Cougars prefer to eat deer, but beaver, rabbits, birds and even mice and frogs are also hunted for food. They sometimes attack cattle.

In midsummer, female cougars give birth to two or three kittens. They are raised only by the mother, and they stay with her for a year.

Swift Fox

The swift fox got its name
From the speed that it could run;
Once common on our prairies,
At present, there are some.

The swift fox liked to dig its den
On land where the grass wasn't tall;
New pups were born each year in May,
But are on their own by the fall.

The swift fox has been declared "extirpated" in Canada. This means that it has become extinct there, though it is still found in other parts of North America. Attempts have recently been made to reintroduce it into southern Alberta and Saskatchewan.

Scientists have had some success releasing a number of these animals back into the wild. Some are surviving and are producing litters of puppies.

This fox is fairly small—about the size of a house cat. It began to disappear when the prairie lands it liked to live on were turned into farms.

It was also killed by traps and by poison intended for wolves and coyotes. Disease may have been another reason for its vanishing from the prairies.

The swift fox keeps its den all year. In this den, the female gives birth to four to six pups each spring.

One odd thing about the swift fox is that it doesn't like windy days, when it will stay in its den.

Vancouver Island Marmot

This small brown marmot likes to live
On a rocky mountainside;
It burrows in among the rocks,
Where it can sleep or hide.

It keeps busy in the summer months,
Eating flowers and fruit all day;
But when September rolls around
It goes to bed till May!

After nine months of hibernation, marmots mate. Then, about one month later, four or five young marmots join the small colony that lives together in a large burrow dug in the ground. Marmots never wander far from their home burrow.

They are playful animals, and two marmots often engage in what seems to be a wrestling match, standing on their hind legs and pushing at each other.

Their favorite food is plants, berries and flowers, which they nibble on just like rabbits.

The only place in the world that this marmot is found is on some high mountains on Vancouver Island. One reason they are endangered is that logging developments and ski resorts are gradually taking over their habitat.

Today, there are fewer than three hundred Vancouver Island Marmots alive.

Whooping Crane

The tallest bird in America
Is called the whooping crane;
Where once it had its breeding grounds,
There now are fields of grain.

These beautiful great flyers
Have wings two meters wide;
They soar aloft on rising air,
Then elegantly glide.

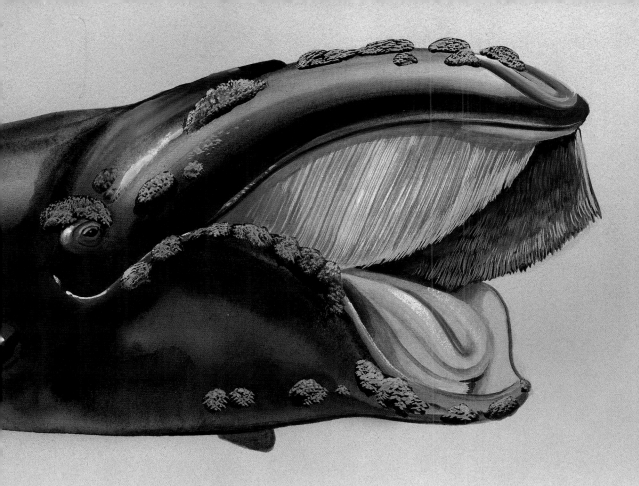

Bowhead whales were hunted almost to extinction. Only a few still swim in the cold northern waters; the number is estimated to be about twenty thousand.

A calf born in the ocean in March or April is about four meters (thirteen feet) long. In time it will grow to be about five times this length and will weigh many, many tons.

These gentle giants have no teeth. Instead, they have comblike plates in their mouths. They feed by taking in huge mouthfuls of water and straining out the tiny sea creatures floating in the water.

Hunting of these whales is now prohibited by all fishers with the exception of the aboriginal peoples.

The bowhead whale's enemies are man, pollution, the orca whale and oil spills.

Sea Otter

Otters are smoothies in the sea,
But clumsy on the land;
Only a very stormy day
Will make them "hit the sand."

Slaughtered for their lovely fur,
They almost disappeared;
But now they've made a comeback,
Though oil spills are feared.

Sea otters do not have a thick layer of fat to keep them warm in the cold ocean, but they do have a warm coat of fur. An oil spill on the coast can be very harmful to sea otters. The oil destroys their fur and they die of the cold.

Many years ago sea otters almost disappeared from the entire west coast of North America. They were hunted for their fur that is so soft and thick that water cannot get through it.

Oil spills, tourists and fishers are among the causes of this animal being endangered.

The small colonies of otters now living off Vancouver Island and other islands along the coast were placed there by conservationists.

Sea otters are about the size of a small dog. They are surviving well off the coast of Alaska.

Sea otters live in kelp beds. They feed on clams, oysters, mussels, crabs and sea urchins.

At night they tie themselves to the kelp so they will not drift out to sea while they are asleep.

Right Whale

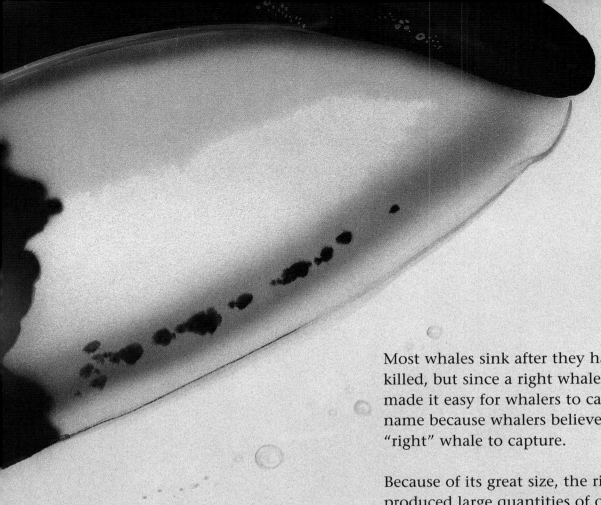

Most whales sink after they have been killed, but since a right whale didn't, this made it easy for whalers to catch. It got its name because whalers believed it was the "right" whale to capture.

Because of its great size, the right whale produced large quantities of oil that was burned in lamps and used to make soap.

As well as being caught by whalers, right whales have been killed when hit by a ship or accidentally captured in fishing nets. In 1946 the right whale was declared a protected species.

The use of so much of the coastal areas by man has caused a loss of habitat for these huge creatures.

This whale was easy to capture
Because it was big and slow;
So whalers thought it was the "right"whale
To hunt many years ago.

There are now only about four thousand right whales left in the oceans of the world. It has few enemies other than man and the orca whale.

Two other features made it the one
For whalers to chase in their boats:
Its blubber is rich in whale oil
And when killed, it doesn't sink, but floats.

A female gives birth to one calf every three to four years. The young calf is nearly five meters (sixteen feet) long at birth.

Leatherback Turtle

Leatherback turtles live in the sea,
But nest on the warm sandy shore;
The female lays great numbers of eggs—
There are hundreds, maybe more.

This is the world's largest turtle;
It can weigh as much as a car;
It travels wherever it wants to,
In the oceans near and far.

Unlike other large turtles, the leatherback does not have a valuable shell. Nor is it hunted for food, since its meat is not thought tasty enough to eat.

Many creatures, including humans, hunt for and eat the its eggs, which are found in sandy nests on the beach. Because of this, not many of the hundreds of eggs that the female lays hatch successfully. This and the killing of turtles for trophies are some of the reasons for their drastic decline.

Leatherback turtles eat fish, sea urchins, seaweed and jellyfish. Plastic bags, which can resemble a jellyfish, are sometimes eaten by the unsuspecting turtle. This is another possible reason for its being endangered.

Leatherback turtles live mainly in the warm oceans, but have been seen as far north as Alaska.

Turtles are the only reptiles with shells.

Blanchard's Cricket Frog

This frog is called a "cricket"
Because of its cricketlike song;
When frightened by an enemy,
The leap it takes is long.

This rare and very threatened frog,
Is found at Point Pelée,
In the province of Ontario,
In a park on Lake Erie.

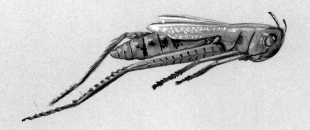

Blanchard's Cricket Frog is a small creature only about three centimeters (one inch) long. When it is frightened it can leap many times its length or skitter quickly across the surface of a pond or lake.

Just before winter this frog, like most northern reptiles, must find a safe place to hibernate. It must burrow into the mud at the bottom of a pond or lake. It must dig deep enough so it is below the level where the ground freezes. If it does not, it will die.

Blanchard's Cricket Frog does not starve during the hibernation because its body does not require any additional food during this time. The food energy the frog stored in its tiny body during the summer will keep it alive during the long hibernation.

Because this frog is so small, it is difficult to find out exactly where it lives and what type of environment it needs to survive.

The female and male frogs of this species are easy to tell apart. The male has a bright yellow-colored throat and vocal pouch, while the female doesn't.

The word *cricket* in its name comes from the sound it makes. The sound is like two rocks being clicked together. This sound is also similar to the chirping of the black cricket.

Like all creatures of the world, the cricket frog must find a safe place to live. Conservationists hope that the breeding sites for this rare frog will be preserved. If this happens, this tiny frog may be taken off the endangered list.

Spotted Bat

Not much is known about these bats—
Small things with massive ears;
Their spots are three—two on their backs
And one upon their rears.

By day they roost on rocky cliffs,
At night they fly about;
If moths are in their neighborhood,
They'd be wise to fly right out.

These bats are easy to spot because they are quite large, with a wingspan of about thirty-five centimeters (fourteen inches). They have black fur on their backs and three large white spots, which give them their name. Their underside is white.

Scientists fear that the spotted bat is threatened both by the use of pesticides, which poison the bats, by forest cutting and by more land being taken by man to build towns.

Bats have very weak eyesight. They navigate in the dark by sending out shrill calls that bounce back to their large ears in the same way that humans use radar.

Bats are the only mammals that can fly. They spend the night flying about catching insects. The spotted bats' favorite food is moths, which they easily catch while flying.

Most bats live in large colonies, but the spotted bats live by themselves. Spotted bats live in western parts of the United States, Mexico and Canada. They are endangered in Canada, where only a small population remains. Most of these live in the dry interior valleys of British Columbia.

Piping Plover

The piping plover builds its nest
On the shore of a lake or ocean;
If anything should threaten it,
This plover will cause a commotion.

Many things threaten the plover,
For their eggs are easy to spot;
If a hungry skunk should find them,
It will gobble up the lot.

When anything approaches a piping plover's nest containing four spotted eggs, the plover puts on an interesting show. It may fly from its nest and flop down on the sand, pretending to be injured. It does this to draw an enemy away from its precious eggs.

One reason the plover is endangered is the place where it builds its nest. This is always just above the high-water mark on a lake or ocean.

If there is a storm or an especially high tide, the plover's nest and eggs will be washed away. Should this happen, the plover will sometimes build a new nest and then try again to hatch and raise the young chicks.

The piping plover is also endangered because people build their homes and cottages too close to their nesting areas.

Piping plovers live in the midwestern parts of Canada and the United States. They also live along the sandy shores of lakes from southern Canada to Nebraska, down the Atlantic coast to Florida, and across Texas to the Gulf of Mexico.

There may be only about two thousand piping plovers alive.

Published by:
Grasshopper Books Publishing
106 Waddington Drive
Kamloops, British Columbia
Canada V2E 1M2

This book is dedicated to my favorite oldest son, John Dwight Mastin.

Acknowledgments:
The author wishes to thank the following: Committee on the Status of Endangered Wildlife, Bats of British Columbia, the governments of Canada and British Columbia, Bill Gilroy of the Kamloops Wildlife Park, Dr. Ken Taylor, UCC.

Designed by Kunz+Associates

Canadian Cataloguing in Publication Data
Mastin, Colleayn, O. (Colleayn Olive)
North American endangered species

(Grasshopper series; 4)
Includes index.
ISBN 1-895910-27-7

1. Endangered species—North American—Juvenile literature.
I. Sovak , Jan, 1953– II. Title. III. Series: Mastin, Colleayn O. (Colleayn Olive), Grasshopper series; 4.
QL84.M38 1997   j591.68'097   C97-910361-4

Printed in Canada